Disney LEARNING

Disney·PIXAR FINDING DORY

AGES

6-7

KEY STAGE 1

Spelling and Grammar

Scholastic Children's Books,
Euston House,
24 Eversholt Street,
London NW1 1DB, UK

A division of Scholastic Ltd
London ~ New York ~ Toronto ~ Sydney ~ Auckland
Mexico City ~ New Delhi ~ Hong Kong

Published in the UK by Scholastic Ltd, 2016.

ISBN 978 1407 16584 4

Printed in the UK by Bell and Bain Ltd, Glasgow

2 4 6 8 10 9 7 5 3

Papers used by Scholastic Children's Books are made from woods grown in sustainable forests.

www.scholastic.co.uk

Welcome to the Disney Learning Programme!

Children learn best when they are having fun! The **Disney Learning Workbooks** are an engaging way for children to develop their spelling and grammar skills along with fun characters from the wonderful world of Disney.

The **Disney Learning Workbooks** are carefully levelled to present new challenges to developing learners. Designed to support the National Curriculum in England: English Programme of Study at Key Stage 1, this title offers children the opportunity to practise skills learned at school and to consolidate their learning in a relaxed home setting with parental support. With stickers, motivating story pages and a range of English activities related to the film *Finding Dory*, your children will have fun while learning about grammar and improving their spelling.

Developing an understanding of grammar will help children gain control of their writing. Once they learn how to structure sentences, they will be able to express their ideas with clarity and cohesion. When children can use grammar effectively, they will also be able to make choices about how they want to structure their writing. This **Disney Learning Workbook** will help children to develop confidence in the key parts of grammar for Year 2, standing them in good stead for the primary school years and beyond.

This book includes 'Let's Read' stories featuring characters from the film *Finding Dory* for you to enjoy together. Keep each session fun and short, and check your child's work periodically to ensure that the activities have been understood and spelling exercises have been completed accurately. Please note that the grammar activities have been devised using the 2014 National Curriculum grammar glossary. Some schools may have been using slightly different terminology in the past, but all schools will be using these new terms from now on.

Have fun with the Disney Learning programme!

Developed in conjunction with Charlotte Raby, educational consultant

Let's Practise Spelling and Grammar

The pages of this book are filled with fun activities to help you practise your spelling and use grammar correctly.

Good grammar helps us to write in clear sentences. This book will show you how to:

★ Create exact descriptions of characters using noun phrases.

★ Use verbs to show time passing in your stories.

★ Use prepositions to show where your characters are.

★ Write sentences using the co-ordinating conjunctions **and**, **or** and **but**.

★ Write sentences using the subordinating conjunctions **when**, **if**, **that** and **because**.

Check your answers on pages 44 to 46.

Ask a grown-up to help you read the instructions if you are not sure what to do.

Dory knows that it's important to keep trying until you get it right. She will help you become great at spelling and grammar!

Say the sentence out loud before you write it down. When you've finished, read it back again. Are all the words there and in the right places?

Use a capital letter at the beginning of each sentence, for the names of people and places, and the word I.

Don't worry if you make a mistake – everyone does when they are learning! Just cross it out and try again.

The Great Barrier Reef was a wonderful place to live. Dory loved the beautiful coral, the warm waters and the amazing sea creatures. Every morning, she would rush out of her cave and say a happy hello to her friends, Marlin and Nemo.

Sometimes, Dory helped Marlin take Nemo to school. The little orange clownfish was in Mr Ray's class. One morning when they arrived, the whole class was excited. Mr Ray explained that he had planned something special for the children. He was going to take them on a field trip to see a migration!

Poor Nemo looked confused. He wondered what a migration could be. When he asked his dad about it, Marlin told him to wait and see. The migration was going to be a big surprise. Marlin said goodbye to Nemo and swam away. Dory stayed to watch.

One by one the children hopped on Mr Ray's back, ready to glide over the coral reef. Dory thought that the teacher wanted her to help him, so she followed, too. Although she sometimes struggled to remember names and faces, she loved to learn new things. She couldn't wait to find out more about the migration.

Mr Ray took the children to a sandy spot, then told everyone to look up. Suddenly thousands of stingrays glided right past the reef! Dory gasped in surprise.

Let's Find Out About Sentences

We use sentences all the time.

Sentences are a group of words that make sense on their own.

They start with a **capital letter** and always include a verb.

They can end with a full stop (.), exclamation mark (!) or question mark (?).

Dory stayed **to watch**.

Read these groups of words.
Can you underline the sentences?

1 the whole class was waiting for them.

2 Poor Nemo looked confused.

3 what a migration could be

4 One by one the children hopped on his back,

5 then told everyone to look up.

6 Dory gasped in surprise.

Do the words start with a capital letter? Do they include a verb and end with a full stop, exclamation mark or question mark? Don't forget to check!

A group of words that gives the reader information, but doesn't include a verb is called a **phrase**.

thousands of stingrays

A **clause** is a group of words that makes sense and **does** include a verb. A sentence is a type of clause, but beware, not all clauses are sentences.

The migration reminded **her of something.**

so she followed

then told **everyone to look up.**

Underline the clauses in this list. One of the clauses is a sentence. Can you circle it?

1   she loved to learn new things.

2   The little orange clownfish

3   Everybody was very excited.

4   all of his students

5   a big surprise

6   he had planned something special

Remember! Every clause must have a verb.

9

Let's Look at Verbs

Verbs make things happen in sentences.

They can end in the suffixes **-s**, **-ing** and **-ed**.

Verbs can be actions, feelings and thoughts. Without them we cannot write about what characters think, do or feel!

Dory loves playing **with Nemo and his friends.**

She thinks **they are lots of fun!**

Underline the verbs in these sentences.

1   Mr Ray teaches Nemo.

2   Mr Ray takes the students on his back when they go on a field trip.

3   The students learn about the creatures that live in the reef.

4   Dory likes helping Mr Ray.

5   They all laughed.

What is Dory doing? Write a sentence about her. Don't forget to use a verb!

10

There are four different types of sentences – statement, command, exclamation and question.

Statements are the most common type of sentence. They give people information.

I'm a whale shark.

Give me your tag.

Commands start with a verb.

Exclamations have an exclamation mark at the end.

Cuddle party!

Questions end with a question mark. Words like what, where and why can often start questions.

What would Dory do?

Can you identify these sentences? Put the right sticker at the end of each line, using the key to help you.

1	Did I forget again?
2	Get off the rock.
3	Hank has three hearts.
4	The undertow is dangerous!

STICKER KEY:

statement

command

exclamation

question

Let's Look at Nouns

In English we have more **nouns** than any other type of word! Nouns give things a name. Nouns can also label ideas and feelings.

Nouns can be **singular**.

Dory **is a** fish **that wants to find her** family.

Dory **has a short** memory.

Sometimes nouns can also be **plural**.

Many creatures **try to help Dory.**

Underline the nouns in these sentences.

1 I put my head under the water.

2 Mr Ray sings songs as he swims with his class.

3 The otters love to cuddle.

4 Hank is an octopus and he lives in a tank.

5 Gerald the sea lion loves to carry a green bucket in his mouth!

6 Bailey is a big, friendly whale.

A **proper noun** begins with a capital letter. Proper nouns name people, places and organisations, like schools. The days of the week and the months of the year are all proper nouns.

On Tuesday **3rd** March, Lisa **and** Frankie **are going to the** Marine Life Institute.

Can you underline the proper nouns in these sentences?

1. Welcome to the Marine Life Institute – people call it the Jewel of Morro Bay.

2. It's the California current, dude.

3. Dory swims to the edge of the Drop-off.

4. Mr Ray teaches all the little fish in his class.

All finished? Give yourself a 'yay' from Mr Ray! Stick his picture here.

Now write your own *Finding Dory* sentence. Don't forget to give the proper nouns capital letters.

- - - - - - - - - - - - - - - - - - - -

- - - - - - - - - - - - - - - - - - - -

Let's Spell Plurals

We use plurals to show that we have more than one of something. We make nouns into plurals by adding the suffixes **-s** or **-es**.

Suffixes are letters added at the end of the word to change its meaning.

Most words are made plural by just adding **-s** at the end of the noun.

friend
noun

friends
plural noun

Add an **-s** at the end of these nouns to make them plural. When you've finished writing, stick in pictures to match the plurals.

1

plant _____
noun   plural noun

2

sea lion _____
noun   plural noun

Some nouns need the suffix **-es** when they are made into the plural. These words end with the sounds ss, sh, zz, ch and x.

fish
noun

fishes
plural noun

Sometimes people use 'fish' for the plural. This is OK, too.

Make these nouns plural by adding **-es** at the end of each one.

3 class _____

4 box _____

5 beach _____

14

Nouns ending in **-y** have their own special rule. To make these words plural, you have to do two things.

First swap the **y** for an **i**.

fl**y** fl**i**

Then add **-es**.

fl**i** + es = fl**i**es

Be careful – some words are out to trick you! At first the word **valley** looks like it should follow the swap rule. But if you look closer, you'll see that the final sound of the word is made with the two letters, **-ey**.

When a noun ends in **-ey**, all you have to do to make it plural is add **-s**.

valley   **valleys**

noun   plural noun

Use the 'swap' rule to make these nouns plural.

6 sky _____

7 city _____

8 family _____

9 story _____

Now practise making these nouns plural.

10 journey _____

11 alley _____

12 key _____

13 monkey _____

Did you know that -ay nouns work like this too?

Let's Spell Words with Suffixes

The most common suffixes are **-ing** and **-ed**. They are called verb suffixes. You probably use them all of the time, without even thinking.

Verbs that end in the suffix **-ing** are in the **present** tense. They tell you that something is happening now.

Verbs that end in the suffix **-ed** are in the **past** tense. They tell you something has already happened.

I am sitting!

I wanted to sleep, but Gerald woke me up!

Stick in a picture of Rudder next to the speech bubble written in the present tense.

Now stick in a picture of Fluke next to the speech bubble written in the past tense.

Most words don't change when you add the suffixes **-ed** and **-ing**.

help ➡ help**ed** ➡ help**ing**

remember ➡ remember**ed** ➡ remember**ing**

wait ➡ wait**ed** ➡ wait**ing**

Not all words work like this, however. When you are spelling, there are some simple rules for adding suffixes.

Every time you want to add a suffix to a word ask yourself this question:

 Do I need to **double**, **drop** or **swap** the last letter of the word?

Some words follow the **double** rule when you add a suffix.

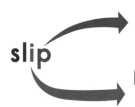

slip

Look at the last letter of the word. Is it a **consonant**?

Look at the letter before it. Is it a **short vowel (a, e, i, o** or **u)**?

Then double the **consonant** and add **-ing**. You are protecting the short vowel sound.

slip → **slipp + ing** → **slipping**

These spellings follow the double rule. Protect the short vowel, then add the suffix **-ing**.

1 swim _____

2 beg _____

3 fan _____

When you've finished, put in a sticker of Dory acting out the verb in question 1.

The doubling rule works when you add the suffix **-ed** to a verb, too. Just double the consonant and add **-ed** to protect the short vowel sound.

Use the doubling rule to add the suffix **-ed** to these words.

4 grin _____

5 bob _____

6 flit _____

When you've finished, put in a sticker of Destiny acting out the verb in question 5.

Let's Spell Words with Suffixes

Sometimes when you add a
suffix, you need to follow the **drop** rule.

hope

Look at the last letter of
the word. Is it an **e**?

Look at the letter before it.
Is it a **consonant**?

Drop the **e** before you
add the **-ing**!

hope ➡ **hope + ing** ➡ **hoping**

These spellings follow the drop rule. Drop the **e**, then add the suffix **-ing**.

1 hide _____

2 slide _____

3 escape _____

When you've
finished, put in a
sticker of Nemo
acting out the verb
in question 1.

The drop rule works when you add the suffix **-ed**, too.

Use the drop rule with these words. Don't forget to drop
the **e** before you add the suffix **-ed**.

4 stare _____   6 love _____

5 dance _____

When you've
finished, put in a
sticker of Hank
acting out the verb
in question 4.

Some words follow the **swap** rule
when you add the suffix **-ed**.

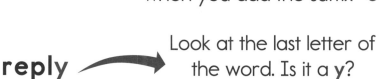

reply → Look at the last letter of the word. Is it a **y**? You need to swap the **y** for an **i** when you add the suffix **-ed**.

reply ➡ reply swap i + ed ➡ replied

Use the swap rule to spell these words. Remember to swap
the **y** for an **i** before you add the suffix **-ed**.

7 ⭐ copy _____

8 ⭐ cry _____

9 ⭐ try _____

When you've finished, put in stickers of some fish acting out the verb in question 7.

When you are adding the suffix **-ing** to words ending in **y**,
there's no need to follow the swap rule. Just add the suffix at the end.

reply ➡ **replying**

Add the suffix **-ing** to these words.

10 ⭐ carry _____

11 ⭐ spy _____

12 ⭐ fry _____

When you've finished, put in a sticker of Dory acting out the verb in question 10.

Let's Learn About the Progressive Tense

Verbs ending in the suffix **-ing**
tell us that the action in the sentence is happening
over a period of time. They are called **progressive** verbs.

Dory looks **for her family.** ➡ The verb in this sentence is looks. It is the present tense, which means it is happening now.

Dory is looking **for her family.** ➡ The verb in this sentence is made up of the two verbs – is and looking. This tells us that Dory is looking now and that she will keep on looking.

	To be (present tense)
I	am
he/she/it	is
you	are
they	are
we	are

If we want to write a story where something happens for a while then we use **am**, **is** or **are** and the verb with the suffix **-ing**.

Let's fill in the verbs and make some sentences. Use the table to help you choose the correct part of the verb 'to be', then add the verb ending **-ing**.

Here's an example to get you started.

Dory is trying **to remember where she** is going.

VERBS: trying and going

_____

1 The sea lions _____

at Gerald's daft antics.

VERB: laughing

_____

2 Marlin _____ for Dory.

VERB: looking

If we want to write about something that was happening in the past, we could write it in two ways.

Dory looked for her family. ➡ The verb in this sentence is looked. It is the past tense, which means it happened and is over.

Dory was looking for her family. ➡ The verb in this sentence is made up of the two verbs – was and looking. This tells us that the Dory was looking for her family for a period of time.

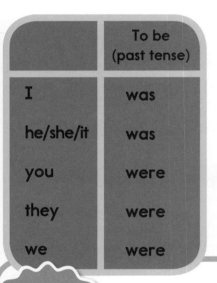

	To be (past tense)
I	was
he/she/it	was
you	were
they	were
we	were

If we want to write a story where something happened for a while in the past then we use **was** or **were** and the verb with the suffix **-ing**.

Fill in the verbs in the **past tense** to make some more sentences. Use the table to help you choose the correct part of the verb 'to be', then add the verb ending in **-ing**.

Here's an example to get you started.

Dory was trying to remember where she was going.

VERBs: trying and going

_____

3 Dory _____ to Destiny.

VERB: talking

_____

4 The hermit crabs _____

the bath toys as shells!

VERB: using

Let's Learn About Homophones

Homophones are words that sound the same, but have different meanings and spellings.

Read the words and find out what they mean, then learn some top tips to help you remember which is which!

1

there

There has the word here in it. It means 'that place'.

their

Their means 'belonging to them'.

they're

They're is a shortened version of 'they are'. The 're shows that the letter a from the word are is missing.

Choose the right stickers to complete the sentence.

We waited over ⬭ , but I don't think ⬭ coming.

2

see

You see with your eyes. The two 'e's in see look like a pair of eyes.

sea

The sea has big waves in it.

Choose the right stickers to complete the sentence.

I can ⬭ dolphins playing in the ⬭ .

3

hear

Hear has the word ear in it. You hear with your ear.

here

Here means 'this place'.

Choose the right stickers to complete the sentence.

"Come ⬭ ," called Dory. "I can't ⬭ you."

4

sun

Is the **sun** up in the sky? We can remember the spelling because it has a **u** in the middle like the word **up**.

son

What parents can call a boy child. It has an **o** in the middle just like the word **boy**.

Choose the right stickers to complete the sentence.

Marvin's ⬭ was called Nemo. Nemo swam to the top of the ocean to see the ⬭.

5

one

One means 'the number 1'.

won

Won is the past tense of the verb 'to win'.

Choose the right stickers to complete the sentence.

Dory had ⬭ chance to win the game and luckily she ⬭!

6

night

Means 'the end of the day', when you go to bed!

knight

A **knight** is a hero in shining armour, who likes to slay dragons! Remember the spelling by saying, 'silly **k**-night'.

Choose the right stickers to complete the sentence.

The ⬭ got onto his horse and galloped into the dark ⬭.

Dory watched the rays glide overhead. Mr Ray warned her about the undertow. She remembered she'd heard that word before. Dory gazed in awe, but suddenly the strong current sucked her into the undertow and everything went black. When she awoke, memories of her parents began flooding her mind. Marlin said she had murmured something about 'The Jewel of Morro Bay, California'. Dory decided to go there straightaway.

A New Friend

Dory couldn't wait to find her family. Nemo and
Marlin swam with her and with the help of Crush the turtle
they made their way across the ocean. But when the friends
finally arrived in Morro Bay, a human in a dinghy scooped Dory
out of the water! The human thought that Dory was in distress.
They decided to take her to the Marine Life Institute nearby.

The humans at the Marine Life Institute clipped a tag on to Dory's
fin. They put her in a tank in a room on her own. Poor Dory
missed her friends, Nemo and Marlin. Before she could work out
what to do next, an orange tentacle plunged into the tank. Dory
looked up. The tentacle belonged to an enormous octopus!

The octopus told Dory that he was called Hank. He explained
that Dory's tag meant she would soon be taken to an aquarium
in Cleveland. The octopus wanted Dory's tag so that he could go
there. Dory promised to give it to him on one condition – he had
to help her find her family. Hank agreed.
They had a deal!

Let's Learn About Noun Phrases

Remember, a phrase does not have a verb in it.

A noun phrase is a group of words that give us more information about a noun.

a very forgetful fish ➤ This is an example of a noun phrase. All the words in the phrase tell us more about the **fish**. It tells us that she is very forgetful.

The old man **in the boat** ➤ All the words in this noun phrase tell us more about the **man**. It tells us that he is old and that he is in the boat.

Underline the noun phrases in these sentences. Here's another example to get you started.

Marvin and Nemo struggled through <u>the maze of yellow and green kelp</u>.

1. Dory is put in a glass tank.

2. A huge, orange tentacle drops into the tank.

3. The tentacle belongs to a big, slippery octopus.

4. Dory stares at Hank with wide, surprised eyes.

It's time to make your own noun phrases!
Use the words on this page to create some new noun phrases about Dory.

How would you describe Dory?

kind

cheerful   forgetful

lost   friendly

What does she look like?

bright blue body   huge eyes

yellow fins

wonderful smile   sparkling eyes

Where is she?

in the coral   among the seaweed

behind a shell   in the ocean

inside an anemone

How long can you make your noun phrase?
Here's an example to get you started:

DON'T use a verb in your noun phrase.

a kind fish with huge eyes behind a shell in the coral

Let's Use Co-ordinating Conjunctions

Co-ordinating conjunctions join up
words, phrases and clauses. There are seven to find out about.

for and nor but or yet so

We are going to learn about the co-ordinating conjunctions
and, or and but.

Dory is a blue and yellow fish.

The **and** is joining the words blue and yellow.

Write and, or or but to join these words.

1 Marlin is not sure if he is coming _____ going!

2 Dory is kind _____ helpful.

3 Nemo is small, _____ he is also mighty!

The **or** is joining the clauses together.

Co-ordinating conjunctions can be used to join up **phrases**.

Do you prefer the deep blue ocean or the warm colourful coral reef?

Write and, or or but to join these phrases.

4 Hank has seven tentacles _____ three hearts.

5 Do you want to paddle, surf _____ run on the sand?

Co-ordinating conjunctions can be used to join up **clauses**, too.

Dory is looking for her family but she doesn't know where to start her search.

The **but** is joining the two clauses.

Write and, or or but to join these words.

6   Destiny waits for Dory, _____ she doesn't come.

7   The otters are very cute _____ they're furry, too.

8   Marlin and Nemo are looking for Dory _____ they don't know where to look.

9   Should Dory stay at the Marine Life Institute _____ should she try to escape?

Clause game

1   Use your stickers to make some clause cards. Stick the clauses onto pieces of card, then ask a grown-up to cut them out.

2   Afterwards, use the **and**, **but** and **or** stickers to make cards as well.

3   When you've finished, try making sentences with the cards. Don't forget to join the clauses with **and**, **but** and **or**. Do all your sentences make sense?

Let's Use Subordinating Conjunctions

There are lots of **subordinating conjunctions**. They join clauses in a special way.

We are going to learn about the subordinating conjunctions **when**, **that**, **if** and **because**.

Dory is looking for her family

This main clause makes sense. It doesn't need any more information.

A clause that has a verb and makes sense on its own is called a **main clause**. All the clauses in the game on page 29 are main clauses.

When Dory is looking for her family

This is now a subordinate clause, because it doesn't make sense on its own. It needs more information.

When you add a subordinating conjunction to a clause it becomes a **subordinate clause**. It doesn't make sense on its own.

Read each clause, then tick a box to say if it is a **main clause** or a **subordinate** clause.

	main clause	subordinate clause
Destiny is a whale shark		
when Destiny was waiting for Dory		
if Hank had been more careful with scissors		
Hank has seven tentacles		
because she wants to find her family		
that means she often gets into trouble		

Clause game   Use your stickers to make some subordinate clause cards.

1 Stick the blue phrases onto a piece of card, then ask a grown-up to cut them out.

2 Join the subordinate clause cards to the main clause cards from the game on page 29. Now you can make complete sentences!

3 Write your favourite sentences here.

Let's Use Prepositions

A **preposition** is a word that comes after a **noun**, **pronoun** or **noun** phrase, linking it to another word in the sentence.

There are lots of prepositions.
They often tell us about the location of things.

Dory is beside **Hank.**

Pronouns are words that replace nouns in a sentence, such as I, me, you, he, she, we or it.

inside

above

Where is Dory? Choose the correct preposition from the bubbles, then write it into the sentences.

below

with

1 Dory is _____ the jug.

2 Mr Ray is _____ the hermit crab.

3 Rudder is _____ Fluke.

4 Nemo is _____ Marlin.

Put some stickers of Dory and her friends into the coral reef. Can you write some sentences about them?

Pick a preposition!

above   inside   below   with   next to   beside   under   behind   over   in front of

Try to use some prepositions to describe where the sea creatures are in the picture.

Let's Spell Tricky Words

Tricky words don't follow the normal spelling rules. How many can you spell from this list?

door	child	cold	break
floor	children	gold	steak
poor	wild	hold	pretty
because	climb	told	beautiful
find	most	every	after
kind	only	everybody	fast
mind	both	even	last
behind	old	great	past

Decide which part of the word is tricky, then draw a circle around it. Now you only need to learn that bit! Make the tricky part stand out by writing it in a different colour.

b (eau) tiful

Break tricky words up into sections, so that you can see the other words hiding inside them.

child - ren

bus - y

gr - eat

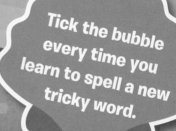

father ◯	move ◯	would ◯	water ◯
class ◯	prove ◯	who ◯	again ◯
grass ◯	improve ◯	whole ◯	half ◯
pass ◯	sure ◯	any ◯	money ◯
plant ◯	sugar ◯	many ◯	Mr
path ◯	eye ◯	clothes ◯	Mrs
bath ◯	could ◯	busy ◯	parents ◯
hour ◯	should ◯	people ◯	Christmas ◯

We say the letters in some words differently to the normal letter sound. When you want to spell a tricky word, say all the letter sounds out loud in the way you want to spell it.

many (we say 'meny')

Say it how you spell it: **man - y**

parents (we say 'pair-rents')

Say it how you spell it: **par - ents**

Use a rhyme to help you remember similar tricky words:

could

should

would

All of these words have the same 'ould' letter pattern.

In the water outside the Marine Life Institute, Marlin and Nemo wondered what to do. They couldn't believe that they had been separated from Dory! The clownfish surfaced by a big rock. Two lazy sea lions called Fluke and Rudder lay there, stretched out in the sunshine. They listened to Marlin and Nemo's story.

Fluke and Rudder promised to help Marlin and Nemo get into the Marine Life Institute. They cooed up to a flock of crazy, red-eyed loons. A bird called Becky was the looniest loon of all. Fluke and Rudder scooped some seawater into a bucket, then put Marlin and Nemo inside.

Becky grasped the bucket in her beak and flapped her wings. Marlin and Nemo were off! The fish felt terrified as they soared through the sky. Suddenly the loon noticed some popcorn spilled across the ground. She hung the green bucket up on a tree branch, then settled down to have a snack.

Marlin tried to get Becky's attention, but he ended up rocking the bucket. The branch flew backwards, flinging the bucket high into the air. Somehow, however, the fish managed to land inside the Marine Institute gift shop. Now all they had to do was find Dory!

Let's Make Sweet Sea Surprises

Pretend that you live in a coral reef, just like Dory! Now make these tasty treats to share with your fishy friends.

You will need:

- 12 ready-made fairy cakes

- 400g buttercream icing, either bought or homemade

- blue food colouring

- 100g plain digestive biscuits

- a mix of sea life jelly sweets and shell shapes

- 12 small cocktail umbrellas

What to do:

1

Put the buttercream icing in a bowl. Sprinkle in a few drops of blue food colouring, then use a wooden spoon to mix it in.

2

Arrange the cupcakes on a clean worktop, then spread a layer of the blue icing over the top of each one. When each cake is covered, use a fork to fluff up the icing so that it forms little blue waves.

3

While the icing is setting, tip the digestive biscuits into a large mixing bowl. Use a wooden spoon to crush the biscuits up into tiny crumbs.

4

Carefully sprinkle a spoonful of biscuit crumbs across one half of each cupcake. Flatten the crumbs down a touch so that they look like sand. Continue adding crumbs until all 12 cupcakes have a little stretch of beach across them.

5

Open up your jelly sweets, then drop one or two amongst the blue icing on the cupcakes. They will look like creatures coming out of the sea! Add some shells, too.

6

Pop a colourful cocktail umbrella into each cupcake. Your sea surprises are ready to serve!

Here Are All the Things I Can Do

Put a **Finding Dory** sticker next to all of the things that you can do!

I can identify ...

the difference between a clause and a phrase

a statement

a question

a command

an exclamation

nouns

proper nouns

noun phrases

present tense verbs

past tense verbs

progressive verbs

I can write ...

sentences using the co-ordinating conjunctions and, or and but

sentences using the subordinating conjunctions when, that, if and because

noun phrases to describe Dory

sentences using prepositions

I can ...

spell plurals using the suffixes -s and -es

use the suffixes -es and -ing correctly for words ending in e

use the suffixes -es and -ing correctly for words ending in y

use the suffixes -es and -ing correctly for words ending in a short vowel and then a consonant

choose the correct homophone to use in a sentence

use a range of strategies to spell tricky words

More Activities to Share with Your Child

⭐ Practise and play

There have been some changes in how your child is taught grammar in Key Stage 1. The 2014 National Curriculum has added some new terminology for schools to teach. Don't be afraid of these new words. They are explained throughout the workbook. Use the activities on the pages to prompt discussions so you can find out what your child already knows.

Afterwards, pick out one of the games suggested below and give it a try. Playing together will help reinforce your child's learning in a fun way.

⭐ Noun or not?

Nouns are the most common type of word in the English language, but sometimes they can be hard to recognise. Nouns can name people, places or things, such as 'child', 'village' and 'car', but they can also label feelings, emotions and ideas, such as 'happiness', 'love' and 'gravity'. A way to test if a word is a noun or not is to put the word into the phrase:

the [noun] is/are great

Take turns to suggest words that could be nouns, and then test the word using the phrase. How many nouns can you find playing this game? Take care, however, as the game doesn't work for proper nouns. Proper nouns have capital letters and are used to name specific people, places or things, such as 'Dory', 'California' or 'Open Ocean Exhibit'.

The longest noun phrase ever

A noun phrase contains all of the words used to give more information about a noun.

It can be words that are in front of a noun:

The tall, silent, shadowy, still figure scared me.

All the underlined words tell us about the figure.

Otherwise the words can come after a noun:

The man sitting in his deckchair was reading a comic.

All the underlined words tell us about the man.

Take turns to add a word each to a new noun phrase. Can you create the longest noun phrase ever? The phrase ends when you add a verb.

The longest sentence ever

Now try making the longest sentence possible. Use the conjunctions from inside this book to help you. Start with something simple like:

Dory was lost but she was not scared, when she thought of how excited she would be to see her family, if …

See if you and your child can build a sentence using all of the conjunctions! Just make sure that each clause has a verb.

Praise good efforts

Learning how to write and spell accurately is the foundation to your child's success in English. It takes time to learn all of the spelling rules. Make sure you reward your child's persistence. Use the top tips on pages 34–35 to help each other remember words that are tricky to sound out. Celebrate each new spelling that you conquer and talk about the words that you find hard to get right. Perhaps your child can teach you a way to remember them, too!

Answers

Page 8

1. the whole class was waiting for them.
2. <u>Poor Nemo looked confused.</u>
3. what a migration could be
4. One by one the children hopped on his back,
5. then told everyone to look up.
6. <u>Dory gasped in surprise.</u>

Page 9

1. <u>she loved to learn new things.</u>
2. The little orange clownfish
3. <u>Everybody was very excited.</u>
4. all of his students
5. a big surprise
6. <u>he had planned something special</u>

Question 3 is also a sentence.

Page 10

1. Mr Ray <u>teaches</u> Nemo.
2. Mr Ray <u>takes</u> the students on his back when they <u>go</u> on a field trip.
3. The students <u>learn</u> about the creatures that <u>live</u> in the reef.
4. Dory <u>likes</u> <u>helping</u> Mr Ray.
5. They all <u>laughed</u>.

Page 11

1. question
2. command
3. statement
4. exclamation

Page 12

1. I put my <u>head</u> under the <u>water</u>.
2. <u>Mr Ray</u> sings <u>songs</u> as he swims with his <u>class</u>.
3. The <u>otters</u> love to cuddle.
4. <u>Hank</u> is an <u>octopus</u> and he lives in a <u>tank</u>.
5. <u>Gerald</u> the <u>sea lion</u> loves to carry a green <u>bucket</u> in his <u>mouth</u>!
6. <u>Bailey</u> is a big, friendly <u>whale</u>.

Page 13

1. Welcome to the <u>Marine Life Institute</u> – people call it the <u>Jewel of Morro Bay</u>.
2. It's the <u>California</u> current, dude.
3. <u>Dory</u> swims to the edge of the <u>Drop-off</u>.
4. <u>Mr Ray</u> teaches all the little fish in his class.

Page 14

1. plants

2. sea lions
3. classes
4. boxes
5. beaches

Page 15

6. skies
7. cities
8. families
9. stories
10. journeys
11. alleys
12. keys
13. monkeys

Pages 16–17

I am sleeping!

I wanted to sleep, but Gerald woke me up!

1. swimming
2. begging
3. fanning
4. grinned
5. bobbed
6. flitted

Pages 18–19

1. hiding
2. sliding
3. escaping
4. stared
5. danced
6. loved
7. copied
8. cried
9. tried
10. carrying
11. spying
12. frying

Pages 20–21

1. The sea lions **are laughing** at Gerald's daft antics.
2. Marlin **is looking** for Dory.
3. Dory **was talking** to Destiny.
4. The hermit crabs **were using** the bath toys as shells!

Pages 22–23

1. We waited over **there**, but I don't think **they're** coming.
2. I can **see** dolphins playing in the **sea**.
3. "Come **here**," called Dory. "I can't **hear** you."
4. Marvin's **son** was called Nemo.

   Nemo swam to the top of the ocean to see the **sun**.
5. Dory had **one** chance to win the game and luckily she **won**!
6. The **knight** got onto his horse and galloped into the dark **night**.

Page 26

1. Dory is put in a <u>glass tank</u>.
2. A <u>huge, orange tentacle</u> drops into the tank.
3. The tentacle belongs to a <u>big, slippery octopus</u>.
4. Dory stares at Hank with <u>wide, surprised eyes</u>.

Pages 28–29

1. Marlin is not sure if he is coming **or** going!

2. Dory is kind **and** helpful.

3. Nemo is small, **but** he is also mighty!

4. Hank has seven tentacles **and** three hearts.

5. Do you want to paddle, surf **or** run on the sand?

6. Destiny waits for Dory, **but** she doesn't come.

7. The otters are very cute **and** they're furry, too.

8. Marlin and Nemo are looking for Dory **but** they don't know where to look.

9. Should Dory stay at the Marine Life Institute **or** should she try to escape?

Page 30

	main clause	subordinate clause
Destiny is a whale shark	✔	
when Destiny was waiting for Dory		✔
if Hank had been more careful with scissors		✔
Hank has seven tentacles	✔	
because she wants to find her family		✔
that means she often gets into trouble		✔

Page 32

1. Dory is **inside** the jug.

2. Mr Ray is **above** the crab.

3. Rudder is **with** Fluke.

4. Nemo is **below** Marlin.

![Finding Dory - Disney·Pixar]

CONGRATULATIONS!

....
(Name)

has completed the Disney Learning Workbook:

Spelling and Grammar

Presented on

....
(Date)

....
(Parent's Signature)